THE
STAR SPANGLED BANNER

☆

Written by FRANCIS SCOTT KEY
during the attack on Fort McHenry,
September 13 and 14, 1814

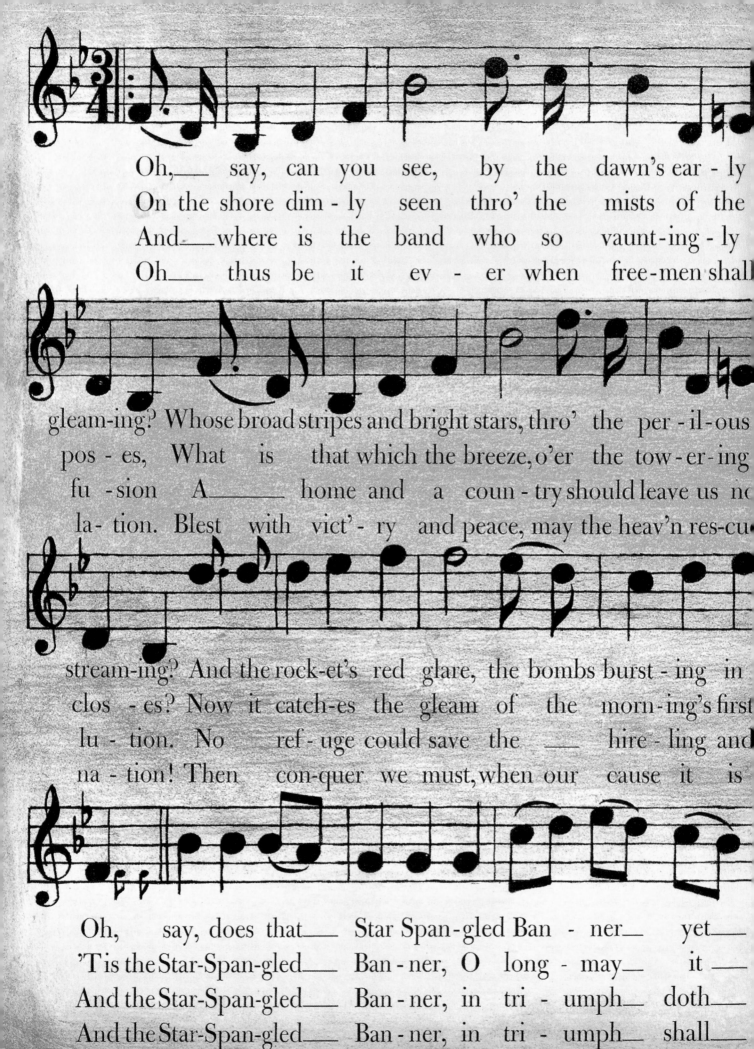

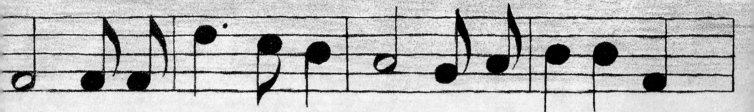

light, What so proud-ly we hail'd at the twi-light's last
deep, Where the foe's haugh-ty host in dread si - lence re-
swore, That the hav - oc of war and the bat-tle's con-
stand Be - tween their loved homes and the war's des - o-

fight, O'er the ram-parts we watch'd were so gal - lant - ly
steep As it fit - ful - ly blows, half con-ceals, half dis-
more? Their blood has wash'd out their foul foot-step's pol-
land Praise the Power that hath made and pre-served us a

air, Gave proof thro' the night that our flag was still there.
beam, In full glo - ry re-flect-ed now___ shines in the stream.
lave From the ter-ror of flight or the gloom of the grave;
just, And this be our mot - to, "In God is our trust."

wave___O'er the land__ of the free and the home of the brave?
wave___O'er the land__ of the free and the home of the brave.
wave___O'er the land__ of the free and the home of the brave.
wave___O'er the land__ of the free and the home of the brave.

Published by Beautiful Feet Books
139 Main Street
Sandwich, MA 02563

www.bfbooks.com
508-833-8626

The Star Spangled Banner

Pictured by Ingri & Edgar Parin d'Aulaire

BEAUTIFUL FEET BOOKS, SANDWICH, MASSACHUSETTS

Oh, say, can you see,

by the dawn's early light,

What so proudly we hailed

at the twilight's last gleaming?

Whose broad stripes
and bright stars,
through the perilous fight,
o'er the ramparts we watched
were so gallantly streaming?

Baltimore - Fort McHenry Sept. 13-14 1814

And the rocket's red glare,
the bombs bursting in air,
Gave proof through the night
that our flag was still there.

Oh, say, does that Star Spangled Banner yet wave

O'er the land of the free and the home of the brave?

On the shore dimly seen

through the mists of the deep,

Where the foe's haughty host

in dread silence reposes,

What is that which the breeze,

o'er the towering steep

As it fitfully blows,

half conceals, half discloses?

Now it catches the gleam

of the morning's first beam,

In full glory reflected

now shines in the stream,

'Tis the Star Spangled Banner, O long may it wave

O'er the land of the free and the home of the brave.

And where is the band

who so vauntingly swore,

That the havoc of war

and the battle's confusion,

A home and a country

should leave us no more?

Their blood has washed out

their foul footstep's pollution.

No refuge could save

the hireling and slave

From the terror of flight

or the gloom of the grave;

And the Star Spangled Banner, in triumph doth wave

O'er the land of the free and the home of the brave.

Oh thus be it ever
when freemen shall stand
Between their loved homes
and the war's desolation.

Blessed with victory and peace,
may the heaven rescued land

Praise the Power

that hath made

and preserved us a nation!

Then conquer we must,

when our cause it is just,

And this be our motto,

"In God is our trust."

And the Star Spangled Banner, in triumph shall wave

O'er the land of the free and the home of the brave.

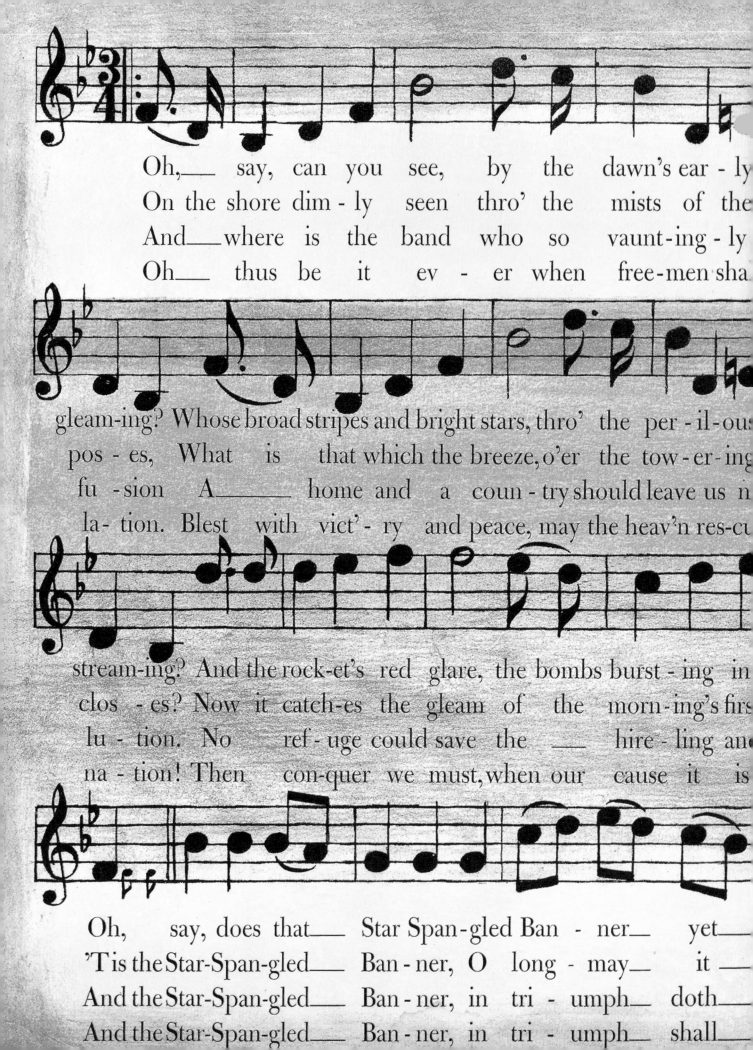

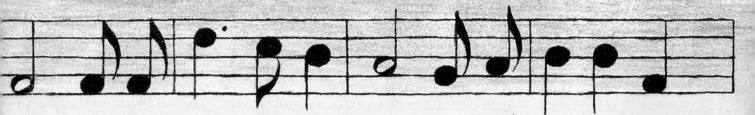

light, What so proud-ly we hail'd at the twi-light's last
deep, Where the foe's haugh-ty host in dread si - lence re-
swore, That the hav - oc of war and the bat-tle's con-
stand Be - tween their loved homes and the war's des - o-

fight, O'er the ram-parts we watch'd were so gal - lant - ly
steep As it fit - ful - ly blows, half con-ceals, half dis-
more? Their blood has wash'd out their foul foot-step's pol-
land Praise the Power that hath made and pre-served us a

air, Gave proof thro' the night that our flag was still there.
beam, In full glo - ry re-flect-ed now___ shines in the stream.
lave From the ter-ror of flight or the gloom of the grave;
just, And this be our mot - to, "In God is our trust."

wave___O'er the land___ of the free and the home of the brave?
wave___O'er the land___ of the free and the home of the brave.
wave___O'er the land___ of the free and the home of the brave.
wave___O'er the land___ of the free and the home of the brave.